© John Brien

DON'T FORGET YER SANNIES!

ISBN 978-0-9927460-1-8

Cover Design, Artwork & Illustrations by Paul Dennis.
www.padnpencil.uk

Published in 2020

LUVULL.COM PUBLICATIONS

CONTENTS

I LOVE THE WAY PEOPLE FROM HULL SPEAK

Just so you know!

Introduction.

Gosh.

That's not really an expression people use in Hull is it? With a few notable exceptions, people tend to use something a bit stronger than that. Well they do, don't they? My excuse is that, although I've lived round here since 1968, I don't actually come from Hull. I love the place; I love the city and I love the way the people speak – hence my first book, *Me Sannies Are Brannies*, was written with genuine affection and was greeted as such by all but a small minority.

It never crossed my mind for even a second that it would be so popular but popular it has been, so, using some of the material left over that I didn't use, some I have since discovered and some that people have kindly given or sent me since *Me Sannies* was published in late 2013, I have, with a mixture of cajoling by family and friends and a confidence I never knew I had until I became a published author and a radio presenter within a few weeks of each other, brought out this second book about the fabulous way people from Hull use that most wonderful of things – the English Language.

A good amount of the help I've been offered by people who've contacted me having read *Me Sannies Are Brannies* has been in the form of words that I hadn't included. I knew I'd be sure to miss out a few but there seem to be nearly as many that I didn't know about as those that I did. Plus of course some that I'd forgotten; I'm quite good at forgetting things. So some of this book will be about those words and, like *Me Sannies*, there will be a kind of glorified glossary where we can see some of the words and, where I've managed to find anything out, something of where and how they originated and, more to the point, whether or not they are unique to Hull.

Before I met my publisher, Paul Dennis owner of LUVULL Publications, PadnPencil.com and the monthly Creative 1 Networking meetings he used to run, I had tried to get other people to publish my book. By the way meeting Paul was thanks to Burnsy on Radio Humberside, though it turned out that we'd known him in the 1970s when he was at Hull College of Art with my wife, Lesley. They do say Hull is the biggest village in the world. I'd spent a long time researching, writing, re-writing, editing and whatever else I did and was determined to get it out there. I wrote twice to a company who publish local books, once actually hand delivering my letter but received no reply, not even an acknowledgement. I also had been in discussion with a national company who publish local interest books all over the UK. I completely rewrote it for them to fit into their house style then they wrote to me saying in effect that Hull didn't warrant a book about its dialect and accent as it wasn't sufficiently different. What do they know? They also said my book would be hard work for the reader and wasn't amusing like their other books. Well they're entitled to their opinion but the response I've had suggests otherwise.

So - as a matter of pure interest - what is it about Hull? According to the people "down south" (and remember I'm from there originally) it doesn't have a dialect worthy of its own book ... just like it wasn't bombed enough in the war to be worthy of TV documentaries. Rant over.

It's good to see that the City of Culture people and their successors are trying to embrace the Hull dialect. When they took their roadshows around the area, the entrance to their tent was emblazoned with the words, "Everyone back to ours", which I didn't get straight away. A brief conversation with one of the volunteers, though, made me realise that those were the exact words that would be said after a party at a local pub or club – the meaning being something like *you're all invited to our house for drinks and nibbles.* I'd really love that to be an expression unique to Hull and, although it is used regularly around here, unfortunately it isn't. It doesn't seem to be in particularly widespread use elsewhere in the country but it's out there. However it's probably more commonly used in Hull than anywhere else so it can be claimed as part of the dialect. Just not solely ours, which is a shame.

As in *Me Sannies Are Brannies* it is vitally important to know, when you read this book, that it is written entirely with my love of the way the people speak in Hull in mind. Any time I might appear to criticise or take the Mick is either tongue in cheek or done with complete affection. Except, of course, for *I aren't.* I so wish Hull people wouldn't say I aren't. However many other words they come up with that I love to hear and talk about, *I aren't* just seems wrong. And I still wonder if GCSE examiners read essays which include that phrase and mark the candidates down for their lack of knowledge of the language. Just one reason why Hull could be low in education league tables.

At this point I must let all you readers know that, in February 2014, I was shocked, yes shocked, by a use of the Hull accent arguably worse than *I aren't.* Yes something worse than the thing I've said several times is the one and only thing I really dislike about the Hull dialect. But it happened. My wife, Lesley, was shopping one day when she heard a woman standing next to her say *I are.* I just don't know what to say about that. Probably enough already. If you're reading this and you have ever said *I are*, please let me know. I won't eat you or even dislike you; I'd just like to know why.

Going back to when I was on my soapbox about people not knowing about the Hull accent, I have a feeling it's because they've never bothered to come and listen. Or maybe it's never entered their heads to think that there might be something here worth listening to. It's amazing how many armchair experts there are whatever your interest. There's never been a TV soap or sitcom made that has been set in Hull so the country didn't get to hear our equivalent of the Likely Lads or The Liver Birds or Till Death do us Part. That's fine for the bulk of the population who don't profess to know about these things but to be unaware of our dialect when you claim to be knowledgeable – that's a crime. I wonder if the City of Culture has made a difference. It'll probably be a few years before we really know what kind of people are visiting the city and where they come from. We'll need to see the long term picture I guess but I'd love to think that the so called language experts would come, see the City and listen to its people.

I could go on until the cows come home about how much I like the Hull dialect. That would take ages but not as long as it would take me to perfect the Hull vowels – particularly the O. I have been on Frome Road when it's been covered in snow and I have bought things for £9.99.

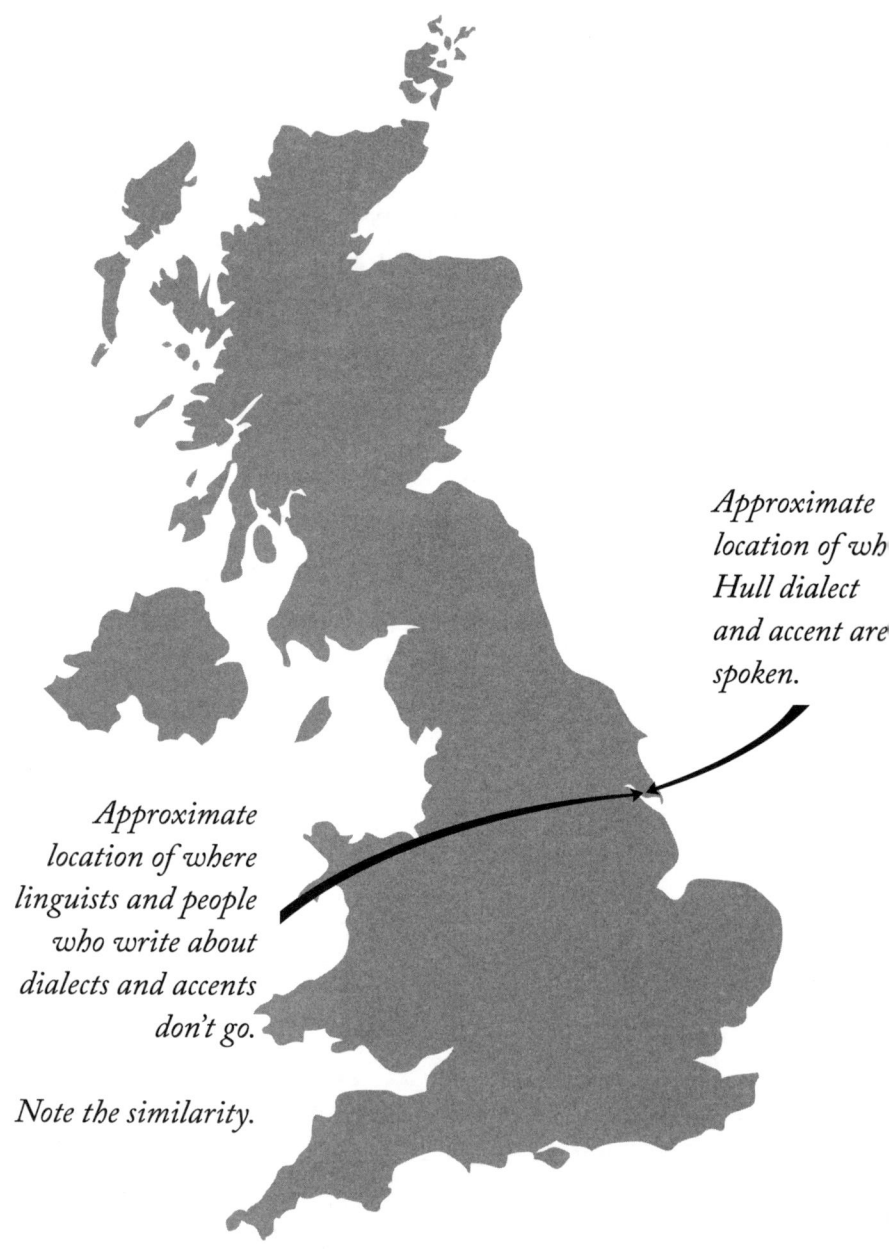

Approximate location of wh Hull dialect and accent are spoken.

Approximate location of where linguists and people who write about dialects and accents don't go.

Note the similarity.

I just say these things a little differently. Alright, a lot differently. Perhaps I'm deprived in not having a strong Hull accent. It's certainly something people should feel proud to possess.

So where do we start on our quest for more niceties about the way Hull people speak?

CHAPTER TWO

NICETIES

I'll try not to repeat myself in this book. I'll try not to repeat myself in this book. But I simply have to state again my favourite Hull word, if only because so many people have said they agree with me. It is the word *while*. My working title for "*Me Sannies Are Brannies*" was "*Don't Cross the Road While You Can See the Green Man*" which, of course, means the precise opposite in Hull to what it does in the rest of the English-speaking world. I love the way Hull people use while when everyone else uses until. Try to keep that in mind until you get to the end of this book. Or should I say while you get there.

Now I've started; and by doing that we're into Hull words and phrases.

One of the things I like is where odd words are missed out but the meaning is still the same. One of my favourites involves the little word by; *It'll be dark by I get home*. Elsewhere it would be *by the time I get home*. Saves a few words I suppose. Another similar one is *I belong the rugby club* or *I belong the choir*. This misses out the word *to* that would be expected. Almost all dictionary definitions (I say that because there's bound to be one that I haven't seen) state that the verb *belong* requires to be followed by a preposition. Lovely isn't it? It just has something special – something that makes it Hull and, like so many other things, a lot of the people of Hull don't realise it, it's so natural. It's a nice little quirky Hull thing but it still makes me sit up and think whenever I hear it.

On the subject of shortening things, we can lurch sideways to another topic in the previous book – that of shortening names. How many of the old night clubs, (mostly now sadly no longer with us) were known as shortened version of their proper names. Welly is still there (The Wellington Club on the corner of Wellington Street) but what about Tiff's (Tiffany's) and Romeo's (Romeo's and Juliet's). And, a repeat I'm afraid, why on earth was the Hofbrauhaus always known as Hoffenbrowse?

All sorts of other things are shortened or amended and have been for many years as this example shows. Speaking to people who were around in the 1920s and 30s, it seems they would buy fish and chips for 3d (old three pence pronounced thrupence throughout the country) but in Hull this could be described as a

2d (Tuppence or tuppenny) fish and 1d (penny) worth of chips or the delightful *Two and One*.

Then there's a really lovely one that Lesley said when I was putting this book together and I've heard it from lots of people before. "I'd better do that bettern't I". *Bettern't I?* - where does that come from?. I can see, though, that it seems a lot less clumsy than *I'd better do that, had I not?* or even *I'd better do that, had I better not?* one of which is probably the correct way, though I really can't be bothered to check as they both sound dreadful. Thinking about it *I think I'd better do that, hadn't I?* would probably be the most common. Research doesn't find a home for this expression, most of the interested people seem to say they've never heard anyone say *bettern't I* or *bettern't you*. I'm not sure that means we can claim it as a Hull expression. I'd like to though, wouldn't you?

Missing letters off names can be interesting too. Yes, I know dropping your Hs is by no means unique to Hull but I really feel sorry for all the girls in Hull called Hannah. So many people will call you Anna. OK so you're a palindrome either way but other names don't get regularly pronounced as if they were another name. Or do they? As I mentioned in *Me Sannies – Doreen* or *D'reen* used to be quite a common girls' name in the area. Yet *Maureen* is never *M'reen* is it – pronounced like *marine?*

A similar thing occurs with the use of *thee* instead of there. Someone might say There's a car coming. To which the reply might be *Is thee?* I quite like this. It's not so very different really from something that's used all over the country – me rather than my – *I'll just get me coat* or *Me dad's gone to the pub*. It's just that saying *thee* in that situation seems pure Hull. I've come across just a handful of people in fifty years living in our part of the world who use *thee* instead of *you* in old West Yorkshire style but I'll stick my neck out and say they are a very small minority.

Similarly you can hear people say – or nowadays see them write on social media – the word *they* instead of there. *Is they a cafe down Whitefriargate?* or *Is they going to be a firework display?* It's kind of understandable as dialect when it's spoken but it always seems strange to me when I see it in writing.

And going back to *thee* leads me to *the*, or more to the point the absence of the word *the*, otherwise known as the definite article. For example, *He's gone to chip shop* or *I'm taking bains to park*. Everybody knows the caricature Yorkshireman and his *trouble at t'mill* – a very slight *t* sound instead of *the* word the and there are variations of this in several pockets of the country from the Lake District to the South Coast. It's known to people who know these things (and have a bizarre language all of their own) as *Definite Article Reduction* or DAR for short but in Hull, as witnessed in the examples I've quoted, there is frequently a complete absence of our friend the definite article which is not recorded elsewhere.

I mentioned certain words that are the same but pronounced differently in Hull. Um-ber-ella is one with its extra syllable, (might you take your Umberella to Witherensea? I wonder) as is mainTAINance rather than MAIN-tenance. I was reminded by my old friend Jo Lewis of the watering hole of the 1970s, the Gondola. I used to hang out there with the good and great of Hull's music scene; lovely memories of rats running across the dance floor. Sorry. It didn't occur to me then but of course it was the Gon-DOE-la not the GON-dola. What would Gilbert and Sullivan have made of that? And nowadays schools, colleges and various other organisations offer pastoral care. I've always known it as PAS-toral but, no, it's pas-TOR-al in Hull.

Then there's the Co-operative - the shop that gave dividends and more recently is allegedly good with food. I've heard that pronounced CORPA-RAY-TIV. It was always the co-op to me and definitely the long name was pronounced co-OP-erative.

Of course Um-ber-ella and With-er-ensea go against all the rules of Hull dialect in that they lengthen words rather than shorten them. I mentioned a few shortenings of names and the like in *Me Sannies are Brannies* but I realise that I forgot at least one. I used to be friendly with a couple of retired East Yorkshire bus drivers. There was always a friendly rivalry between their colleagues and their equivalents at the concern that has successively been Hull Corporation Transport, Hull City Transport and Stagecoach but these two guys always referred to them as *Corpo*. Sounds too much like a character from *Last of the Summer Wine* to me but Corpo it was.

I do know quite a few local musicians across several genres of music. Two of the more prominent are Al Kilvo (Kilvington) and Johnny Pat (Patterson). What else could we expect?

Oh and how many people say *Princess Quay* rather than *Prince's Quay?* There's a subtle difference there. The old Prince's Dock was named in honour of Prince Albert not one of his daughters but so many say *Princess.* Even the long time, (now retired and moved away from the area) manager, Mike Killoran, a really nice man, used to say *Princess Quay.* Nobody dared take him up on it for fear of upsetting him. As I say, he was too nice for that. I do however have to thank a lady called Katie Kingsbury for this photograph of a till receipt from, shall we say, a well-known retailer. Princess Keys!! Nuff said I reckon.

Soon after I started work in Hull I started to get to know the industry jargon. There were names for parts of a building, parts of a lorry or a bus and things used to make everything from caravans to shop fronts to toilet cubicles. One that always stood out to me was a *lath*. I soon discovered that it was a word used for a length of wood (or in our case metal) that was used, usually with other similar pieces, to build up a framework, for example in a hollow wall. What caught my eye – no I should say what caught my ear – was the fact that, though spelt with TH at the end, it was pronounced LATT. I didn't think twice about it at the time, though obviously it found itself a little nook in my memory, as, when I was researching this book, *Lath* was on the long list of words and expressions sent to me by Simon Green at Hull Libraries, some of which my research confirmed were pure Hull. I decided to take *Lath* further and do some research. No that's I lie – I asked one of my former colleagues to do some research which he did by asking both current employees and customers. The answer seemed to be that it is pronounced Latt in Hull and very few other places though we know someone from Liverpool who says *Latt* but he's lived in Hull for quite a few years. Then I Googled *lath pronunciation*. Well, according to both the Oxford and Cambridge dictionaries, it's LARTH – rhyming, of course with how people like me say the word *bath*. Generally, though, the consensus is LATH rhyming with Math or Cath. But it's Latt in Hull. Great.

There is an interesting variant in Hull of the word flag. Not in its meaning as something you fly on a ship or to identify with a country or a sports team but using the word flags as a shortening of flagstones. Flagstone is a type of sandstone rock that appears naturally in a flat form and was used in early stone built buildings to make the floor or the roof. This then kind of evolved to mean any kind of floor or paving stone, which is the Hull meaning. It isn't unique to Hull, far from it in fact but I've included it because it was used a lot in the past by housewives who used to *clean the flags* when they *swilled the passage*. It also gave its name to one of Hull's biggest buildings from the industrial revolution – High Flags Mill. This building was owned and operated by the old Hull company Chambers and Fargus, who, along with three other companies comprised an important industry in the city for many years in which they imported oil seeds and crushed them to make, among other things vegetable oils for margarine, cooking fat, soap and paint. The story goes that High Flags Mill was named after High Flags Wharf, which in turn was named after the massive paving slabs that were laid on the riverbank to facilitate the unloading of barrels of oil. There is, as I write, a business called High Flags Garage on Green Lane, off Wincolmlee. I wonder if they began life near to High Flags Wharf. They'd only have had to move about 200 yards.

Did you ever watch The Professionals on television? Did you notice that, whenever Bodie or Doyle got a call on the radio to go somewhere, their car was always facing the wrong way? Do you think Hull people are always facing the wrong way? Why? Well how often do you hear it said, "So I turned to him and said..." and "He turned to me and he said". Yes we do like to turn to someone and say something when we're recounting a story or even a little incident. This expression is used elsewhere but it seems to be most common in and around Hull so I reckon we can claim it as part of the dialect don't you?

In my first book I spoke about how the present participle is used in Hull. I mentioned, "Do you want serving", asked by a shop assistant but more than once I've rung a company and been asked, "Who are you wanting to speak to?" The rest of the population would be most likely to say, "Who do you want to speak to?" The French can't teach us much about language but they have this right – they have one present tense for verbs so *je parle* can be translated as I speak, I do speak or I am speaking. You wouldn't get that in Hull.

Every so often whilst I was writing both this book and *Me Sannies Are Brannies,* I came across a word or expression that I could not find anything about. I mentioned just now the list of words and expressions I received from Simon Green at Hull Libraries and one turn of phrase on there I passed by several times as I thought there was no way that it was a Hull expression. Eventually I decided to research it and found...nothing. Not a sausage. The expression is to *Have a lot off.*

It's a bit difficult to define but, simply, I think it means someone is having too much to say about something. It might be described as having a rant about something perhaps like we see with footballers disputing a free kick or a corner or the former tennis player John McEnroe who was famous for his rants but it seems to apply equally with a schoolboy being cheeky or having rather too much to say to his teacher. I asked a few people about this expression and the best description came from my younger daughter Anita's old office when she worked in the East End of London. They said that to have a lot off meant to have a fairly drastic haircut. Just a bit different.

There is also the phenomenon of using the wrong word in a situation. Many readers will not be aware that Hull has one of the most successful model railway clubs in Great Britain. They have produced exhibition standard models consistently for decades and have recently celebrated their 70th anniversary. However their name is entirely wrong – they are the Hull Miniature Railway Society. Now there is a distinct difference between a model railway and a miniature railway – for a start you can ride on a miniature railway whereas model ones are generally much smaller and built onto a baseboard. As far as I can ascertain, this is unique, not only in this country but in the world. It could only happen in Hull couldn't it?

Here's a good one though. Early in 2020 Steve Smith wrote on the One Hull of a City Facebook page, "Is it dint or dent? I've always said dint." That, of course, intrigued me and I decided to look it up. A lot of replies, as often happens, stated it was dint in Hull but dent everywhere else. I've certainly heard both used and they seem pretty much interchangeable but what a surprise I got. It seems both words are derived from Old English but that dint was the one in common usage and dent came as a later alternative with absolutely no regional dialect variation.

Finally in this section - which is it; Lawn Mower or Grass Cutter? We've had this discussion in depth within our family and it seems that, in general people in Hull say Grass Cutter. I've always said Lawn Mower but I'm a Southerner by birth as were my parents and grandparents. My daughter-in-law, Eleanor, says Lawn Mower too and she was, like me, born in Brighton. Delving into it, it seems that the lawn mower was invented in Stroud in Gloucestershire n 1830 and was given that name. A grass cutter, at that time, was a person employed, possibly a slave, to cut grass to make hay for horses. It is only relatively recently that it has come into common usage as a machine. It's not a Hull word, though, as I said, grass cutter seems in general use in Hull.

C H A P T E R   T H R E E

PLACES

There are a few more place names that have interested me in the five or six years that have elapsed between books. One that I should have put in the first book is the *Ghost Estate*; or rather *Ghost Estate* as, of course, the *the* is rarely if ever used. I believe it's correctly known as the Mizzen Road Estate and should have a better name than that because all the roads are named after parts of a ship. But for one reason or another, possibly because there was a problem with the drainage, meaning people couldn't get mortgages, the place lay empty for some time after the houses were built and it became known as Ghost Estate; a name which has stuck. I said we don't like change, didn't I?

Then there's Saltshouse Road in East Hull. That's what it's called on the street maps and on the front of the buses but nobody pronounces the middle one of the three Ss. To add to the confusion, there is Salthouse Lane in the City Centre – without a middle S.

Hull is very well provided with parks (by which I mean large areas of green with facilities or at least space for games, picnics etc., not just children's playgrounds (which are known as parks in several parts of the North of England). There are the excitingly-named East Park and West Park and there are others named after people, usually the benefactor who donated the land to be made into a park such as Pearson Park (often incorrectly called Pearson's Park), though presumably not Princess Elizabeth. Then there is Pickering Park – or Picky Park as it is affectionately known to the Hull people who, as we know, love to shorten names.

CHAPTER FOUR

SANNIES

My introduction to the Hull dialect and the reason behind the titles of both of my books on the subject came from the use of the word *Sannies*. Both covers depict them in black but I have to thank Steve Smith for enlightening me to the fact that for special occasions there were also white ones. Thinking about it *ones* is the wrong word to describe shoes but white ones there were. St Mary's High School for Girls for example (now called St Mary's College of course) required the girls to have a pair of *white lace-up sand shoes* for playing tennis. White would also be the preferred colour for trips to the seaside (With-er-en-sea?). For both circumstances there would be a requirement to keep the *sannies* clean. Days out would require smartness and there would be a degree of pride in preparing for a day at the seaside. Anything less than perfect white for school, though, would (at St Mary's at least) risk incurring the wrath of some vindictive nun. There was a substance that rejoiced in the name of Blanco or you could use Kiwi as in the illustration here.

C H A P T E R   F I V E

PHILOSOPHY

I think as well as words and phrases I'll look at some of the attitudes used as well. We are a city with a fairly conservative – with an extremely small c – population. As I said, with a handful of exceptions we know what we like and we don't want to change. This can, of course, be good as we all understand the thing about "change for change's sake". There is no need to change sometimes but other times there really is. If something has become dangerous or something new comes in that is obviously better than what has existed up to now then the argument for change (or modernisation) is pretty much unanswerable. However there are still people who write to the papers or ring radio phone-ins with complaints about what it was like "in my day". Surely if they are still alive and sufficiently *compos mentis* to write or ring, then it still is their day and they should embrace it.

This deeply-entrenched dislike of change in Hull sometimes manifests itself in the expression *If it ain't broke, don't fix it* but we sometimes fail to realise that something is broken. Take all the work done in the city centre in 2016 in preparation for 2017 and the City of Culture. I'd love to have had a pound for every person who complained about it but closed their eyes to how much better (and indeed safer) the whole city centre would become after it was finished. And has.

We can all think of a way that the work could have been done better, faster or causing less disruption. Yes we can! But isn't it just like we can all pick the best team for Hull City, Hull FC or Hull Kingston Rovers. Or any other team of our choosing?

It's the same outlook as the one that didn't want a new hospital when Hull Royal Infirmary was built and, more recently, the Hull Women's and Children's hospital. Please don't tell me that the old Hedon Road maternity home was better. It may have had a lovely atmosphere or ambience and it quite probably had some lovely staff but could it really provide the help and care that the new place can give?

CHAPTER   SIX

FOOD

I went on at length in my first book about certain Hull foods. Patties, Pikelets etc. and there are more of course. Being a musician rather than an author, I was fascinated quite a few years ago when I discovered a shop near to where I used to work that rejoiced in the name of The Bacon Banjo. I was a little sad when

I read that it had closed down after 50 years trading. It took quite a while before I cottoned on to the fact that some Hull people referred to a bacon sandwich as a banjo. I think it referred to any hot sandwich but I stand to be corrected. Strangely, if you went there you got a banjo but if you went to the cafe on the corner you got a bacon cake and further down the road you got a bacon sarnie. How did someone like me know what to ask for in which shop? As a teenager in my first job, I struggled to cope with the concept of a buttered cake (meaning buttered breadcake not fruit cake with butter and/or cheese) but I ate them, probably because everyone else did and the firm I worked for were not over generous with the heating in the office so a hot cake at about 10.00am was often welcome on a cold day. In fact, in the winter, it was even worth offering to go to the cafe for them as it was usually warmer in the queue there than in our office. This was particularly true in the days of Edward Heath's three day week, when we weren't allowed to take two days a week off like everyone else; we had to work those two days with no electricity, just candles. Yes that was the 20th century.

At that cafe they seemed to use an amazingly large amount of what was rather enthusiastically called butter but was more likely to have been the cheapest margarine you could get from the wholesalers but, looking back, that probably helped initiate me into the Hull way of life and I feel I should be grateful for it. (It was about ten years after that that I was officially diagnosed as having IBS!) Even when I stopped working in Hull in 2008, the guys on the shop floor would still solemnly get their *cakes* at morning break; Bacon, sausage, egg or whatever, or the mixture of everything in large amounts that bears the name of a *Belly Buster*. Several cafes in Hull now offer this delicacy and there is now no need to ask what it is. It reminds me of a hotel we stayed at in Cornwall in the 1970s where guests were offered *Full House* for breakfast. We all soon learned that it meant Full English Breakfast but it was never called that.

I ought to mention sherbet at this point. Not food as such but something you put in your mouth allegedly for an enjoyable taste. I wrote in *Me Sannies are Brannies* about Spanish and what I called Kaylie just to get the pronunciation right. This photo I was given anonymously suggests that it might be Kali.

One thing I never realised until comparatively recently, despite all the research and all the people I talked to and listened to when I first started to write, was that Chip Spice is a Hull thing. OK it's a variation on a theme. In the USA they have a number of things they call Seasoned Salts – basically what it says on the label, salt with some seasoning - but the mixture with mainly paprika and tomato powder seems to have been invented in Hull. Whether it's actually made here is a matter for conjecture – it seems not - but the important thing is it originated here. Why, though do the labels all say *American* chip spice? It's no more American than I am and, if it was, it would surely be called *Spice for Fries* wouldn't it? – the Americans call chips fries and chips to them are what we call crisps. You didn't until recently seem to be able to buy chip spice anywhere else in the UK so we can justifiably claim it as our own. I've since discovered (and this rather disturbs me) that Chip Spice is manufactured in Hertfordshire. What's that about? That's as bad as Cadbury's chocolate being made in America. At least the manufacturers acknowledge its roots on their website and are proud to state that it is available from at least two of the well-known supermarkets in the Hull area with one stating that it intends to expand its sales into other parts of the country. I wonder how they choose which parts. There's nowhere quite like Hull as we all know, so they can't use the usual demographics that you find in market research.

I do find it interesting that Hull appears to be the only place in the country where it is difficult to get cod in a fish and chip shop. I've been told in several places around this area that, "You can't get cod", or "It's too expensive", yet in plenty of other places it's the fish of choice, the norm in fact, often followed by plaice. So many fish and chip shops in Hull and the surrounding area only sell haddock which, by the way, I don't like. Several shops just sell "fish" with the assumption that it is haddock; some even give you a strange look if you even ask what it is. There must have been a reason why they spent so much effort on the old fish dock sorting the fish into species for the markets and the trains that went to other parts of the country. It can't have been just Hull people who didn't care can it?

Whilst we're on the subject of food, what do you call your meals? I mentioned breakfast earlier on and there's no arguing about the name for this, just how to say it. Yes, what do you call the first meal of the day? Breakfast of course but in Hull a lot of people, though not all, say BRAKE-fst. Actually of course that's correct as, by eating it, you are breaking your fast but I can't find any evidence of this pronunciation anywhere; not even in slang dictionaries. The norm is definitely BRECK-fst. There is no argument over the second syllable which is pretty much universally pronounced fst with, in effect, no vowel. But do we go for Brake or Breck?

The real difficulty seems to arise over mid-day and evening meals. Rarely is the mid-day meal called lunch. Unless of course you ring somewhere at 1 o'clock to be told that the person you want to speak to is, "On his lunch", or of course "On her lunch".

Sounds uncomfortable to me. Sometimes he/she will be "On his/her dinner", for dinner is the usual term for what you eat in the middle of the day.

Dinner in a lot of the UK is the main evening meal; (My cousin, who lives in Surrey, calls it *Supper* but that's another story, nothing to do with Hull so we'll ignore it). In Hull you normally eat your *tea* at this time of day. I was brought up to call toast and jam or sandwiches in the late afternoon or early evening *Tea* but I've become accustomed to using the word *tea* to describe my main meal of the day if I eat it in the evening. Gosh it's complicated and, unfortunately it's not a Hull thing. I'd love it to be but tea is the name of the main evening meal throughout most of the Midlands and North of England. According to some sources it is a working class expression. Oh well, good for them.

Incidentally when I was young and lived in Sussex, we sometimes went to a café on the seafront at Hove for *High Tea*. That was something like poached eggs on toast. I'm actually shaking my head as I type this which probably says it all. Until very recently I don't think I'd heard the expression *High Tea* spoken in Hull, though the table on a slightly higher level in Coffee 31 in Waltham St. in Hull is referred to as the High Tea Table.

C H A P T E R   S E V E N

WORDS

As in the first book, even though we're only just past half way through, I'm going to edge towards the end of this one with a list of words that may or may not be unique to Hull. Some certainly are, others are not but a significant number are thought of as "Hull speak", so we'll include them because, though not unique to the city, they constitute an important part of the dialect.

Ace. This was a word that I came across with its Hull meaning very soon after we moved to the area. Almost at the same time as I first heard the expression *Me Sannies Are Brannies* in fact. Of course I know the playing card but I'd never heard it used as an adjective before. It means, as I very soon learned, really good, excellent, brilliant or any number of similar words or expressions. Girls at school would say their favourite pop star was *Ace*. I once overheard myself being referred to as *ace* but I never found out why or what it was that I was *ace* at. I didn't dare ask. The word I had used up to then in my home in Hampshire was *peach*. You still hear *That was a peach of a goal* in football commentaries rather than *it was an ace goal* but what can we expect? Someone from elsewhere to use a Hull expression? No, it wouldn't happen would it?

Brock. Every so often whilst I was writing the book something came up which, when I researched it, the result was pretty much exactly the opposite of what I expected. Brock is a word used in Hull to mean *broken* and I just had it firmly in my mind that it was used all over the place just as a regional variation of broken but that seems not to be the case. Brock can mean a badger or it can be a kind of Adonis – a hunk of a man that women fall for left, right and centre. Nowhere – and I mean nowhere – can I find it meaning broken. So, entirely by surprise, we'll claim it as a Hull word.

Christmas Box. I remember being a bit surprised to hear people referring to a Christmas present as a Christmas box. *I bought me mam a necklace for her Christmas box.* In the south a Christmas box is what you might give to certain people in a similar way to giving a tip. One dictionary describes "a present given at Christmas for services during the year". Some people give to their paper boy, their window cleaner or even their dustman. Stop right there, John! Dustman? - should it be binman in Hull? Anyway, remember the Lonnie Donegan song *My Old Man's a Dustman?* One line goes, "Some folks give tips for Christmas and some of them forget. Next time my old man goes round there, he leaves some on the step". In Hull, in the 1970s certainly, you would buy a Christmas box for your mother. Brilliant!

Chudding. This is the Hull word for what is or is not, depending upon your point of view I suppose, an act of dishonesty. The most common word used in the rest of the English-speaking world is *scrumping*. Basically it means going into somebody's garden, field or orchard and taking apples leading, in some cases, to the production of a drink called *Scrumpy*. The word *scrumping* seems to be pretty widespread throughout the UK and America and there is a vast amount of discussion on the subject both in books and on the internet. Other languages have words for it, for example *Epleslang* is the Norwegian word but what is interesting (well it is to me) is that in some places it refers to taking only apples whilst in other places it can also apply to pears and in yet more places it can be any fruit. West Yorkshire claims it for rhubarb by the way. The basic definition seems to be that the apples are collected for personal rather than commercial use. The important thing to us is that everyone else says *scrumping* whilst *chudding* is only used if you speak with a Hull dialect. Just to add to the confusion, though, I have seen it written as *trudding*. Let's leave it as *chudding* shall we.

Courting. If I had a pound for every time I heard somebody ask somebody else, "Are you courting?" I'd be a rich man. Courting is quite an old word dating in fact from the time when the bible was first translated into English when, generally speaking, relationships between couples were – shall we say – more formal and controlled than they are nowadays. The word still exists and is used worldwide but its use in Hull with the meaning, "Are you going out with anyone?" seems to have outlived this definition everywhere else. I was quite shocked when I first heard it as I remember thinking that *courting* meant something a lot more than *going out with*. Some people of my generation still describe the period when they were courting, meaning before they were married; I guess that is decreasing as more and more people live together.

I can't help thinking of the song by the Shangri-Las, *Leader of the Pack*. It begins with two schoolgirls chatting and one saying to the other, "Is she really going out with him?" You know the one. It wouldn't have the same oomph to it if she said, "Are they really courting?" would it ?

Incidentally I have to throw in an expression here from West Yorkshire that I really loved when I heard it and I had to ask what it meant. I used to work with a lady from Bradford who talked to me about when she and her husband were "bothering with each other". What this meant was they were seeing each other but were both still married to someone else. I don't know if there's a Hull word for this.

Frame Up. I personally haven't come across this one but at a couple of talks that I've given people have told me that "Frame Up" is something that would be said meaning "Pull yourself together". It's probably not politically correct to say it nowadays but allegedly it might be said, for example, to me, if I was nervous before doing one of the talks I mentioned. Someone would say "Pull yourself together and get out there". It also can be used to ask or tell someone to stop crying. Apparently in the West

Riding of Yorkshire they say "Frame yourself" or "Frame thissen".

Fussed. Bothered, concerned about something. Normally only used in the negative, for example *Are you pleased that Hull City won? I'm not fussed.* Thinking about it I would say always used in the negative. You wouldn't say I was *fussed* about the football results so -

Fussy. In a similar way – but denoting positiveness - to be fussy about something means to be pleased, even excited about it. *She was really fussy about her new dress.*

Goodies. I mentioned the word *goodies* in *Me Sannies Are Brannies* and its use to mean sweets or what the Americans call *candy*. I've often wondered if there's a connection with the French word *bonbon* – literally good good – which is a type of sweet. Then, more recently, I got involved in a conversation with a man who insisted that the word comes in fact from Swedish and was brought over either by Vikings some long time ago or merchant seamen more recently. If I were to believe either it would be the more recent and that it is possibly derived from the Swedish word *gudis* or *godis*. This might be the name of a shop as suggested by the man who told me. Alternatively it could be a trade name like Cadbury's – I haven't been able to find out which. Have a look at the pictures and if you can understand Swedish please let me know. If you Google Godis and click on Translate this site you get Candy. American of course but in there is a suggestion that the history of the word is derived from good or even goodies. Confusion would appear to reign. You also get this though.

There you go – a bit of Swedish. *Julgodis, påskgodis, Alla hjäärtans dag eller bara vanligt lördagsgodis.* Loosely translated this means Christmas sweets, Easter sweets, Valentine's day or just ordinary sweets. None of which really solves our problem of whether Godis is a company or a general description. The writing under the blue Godis is *Allt du behöver veta om godis och choklad!* Again roughly translated this means All you need to know about sweets and chocolate. Not a lot of help there either.

Grafted.   Normally this is the past tense of a verb meaning to work hard– *he grafted all day in the garden until it was tidy.* But I've come across its use in Hull with a different meaning – filthy dirty – so he might be *grafted after he had grafted,* if you get my drift.

Jawm or Jorm. This is the Hull pronunciation of Jamb, which elsewhere is either said like either *Jam* or *Jarm*. Occasionally it is *Joam*. I think this is a record – 4 ways of saying the same word – and all it is, is the wood (or plastic I guess) around a door.

Knock Off Ginger. This is an interesting one as it has names all over the country; All over the world in fact. It's the Hull name for the children's (or inebriated people's) game of knocking on someone's door and either running away or hiding so, when the door is opened, there's nobody there. Some of the names are quite similar – Knock Off Ginger appears to be special to Hull but it's Knock Down Ginger in London and Knock Up Ginger in South Wales and a few other places. I could almost write a book on this one there are so many alternatives. A few show their faces in different areas of research including Cherry Knocking or simply "Knock Door Run". The ginger bit is strange, especially as it appears all over the place.

Allegedly there is an old English poem which – with the various dialects taken out – goes

> *Ginger, Ginger broke a window*
> *Hit the window - crack!*
> *The baker came out to give 'im a clout*
> *And landed on his back*

All this just to annoy old ladies. And we think today's teenagers are bad.

Made Up.   This is nothing to do with cosmetics that people put on before they go out. Incidentally I remember shortly after I moved to East Yorkshire, I went on a school trip to Snowdonia (yes I did climb Snowdon) and was completely amazed by the transformation of the girls' faces when they put on their make up in the evenings. But I digress; Made up in Hull means pleased, or perhaps similar to the expression *chuffed* that is used in other parts of the North. *He was made up when he heard he'd won the prize.* It's possibly the opposite of *fussed* that we had earlier.

Nithered.   This is quite an interesting word. Well it is to me; I can't expect all of you to share my obsession with such things. Nithered is used in Hull as an adjective meaning cold. If you do just a bit of research though, you will find that *nither* is accepted as a "Northern dialect" word but as a verb meaning to shiver. Maybe we've just evolved a bit more in Hull.

On a Night.   During the evening. Someone may work on a night or may go clubbing *on a night.* It kind of assumes regularity. Despite the use of a night, it implies every night or so many nights a week not just the one.

Out of town.   Anywhere other than Hull itself. So, because I live in Beverley, I come from *Out of town.* People come from *Out of town* to the Freedom Festival or to Hull Fair. When I worked in Hull I was the first person to come to work by train which I occasionally did to the consternation of some of my colleagues some of whom didn't understand why I should want to work in Hull and live *Out of Town.* and others who had never been on a train. On a different subject, when I was thirteen we had a family holiday to Guernsey where we were intrigued by the buses which just said "Town" on the indicator. Irrelevant to this book of course but I found it interesting.

Reurring. I know we should never assume but I must in this case assume there is a relationship between this word and *roaring* if only when that is given a Hull pronunciation. It means crying and does appear to be unique to the Hull dialect. It appears in that worthy son of the city Tom Courtenay's book, "Letters From Home", where he refers to the fact that his father disliked him crying. I hadn't heard of this word until quite recently so possibly it has gone out of general use in the last few years.

Rive (past tense rove). To pull something out. The one I heard was *She's had her kitchen rove out.* Meaning of course she's had a new kitchen installed and the old one removed. Rive, with a different past participle, has a meaning in more standard English as in *a country was riven apart by civil war.*

Sea Roak or Sea Roark. Again pronounce it as you will. It's a mist or fog that comes from the sea, often appearing as merely a wet atmosphere. You know – the type of weather when you don't want to be wearing anything woollen as the wet sticks to it. It seems to have its origins in Scandinavia, as both Swedish and Norwegian languages have a similarly-pronounced word, spelt *rök* in Swedish and pronounced *roik.* Well something like that. Here it's often used instead in the more general North of England expression *Sea Fret*.

Sham Four. This is another word I was introduced to this expression by Simon Green from Hull Libraries. We'd met a few years earlier on the Hullness project and following our discussion he sent me a list of words that people claimed to be special to Hull. A fair bit of the research in this book is thanks to information that Simon gave me for which I am grateful. He has spent some time investigating the phenomenon that is the Sham Four but has never been able to find a printed definition of the term. Basically it is a small house, usually I believe a two-up two-down house that has a scullery which, at the time, was not considered to be a room Simon has studied the databases of local newspapers, searching for 'sham four', and, much as he expected, "all the references are to articles or letters referring to the Hull area, so it is clearly a very local term." He has also found an index card in a staff information file in Hull Reference

Library, which he estimates to be at least 40 years old, making the expression over 100 years old. My research described elsewhere took me to the Hull Daily Mail for 2 July 1935 when a Sham four was being offered for rent. It seems a bit of a derogatory word so it's a little surprising that it should be used when trying to sell house. Nowadays I suppose an estate agent would call a sham four as "deceptively spacious with 4 good sized rooms".

Sink.   A sink can be in the kitchen or it could be what you might do if you can't swim. Both of these definitions occur in just about every dictionary of the English language. However in Hull there seems to be another – a sink is just about any piece of metal that appears in a road and is intended to help water drain away. It might be a manhole cover or a gully or a drain cover in the gutter or any piece of what is colourfully but correctly known as *ironwork*. You sometimes see signs stating *Caution Raised Ironwork* or words to that effect. It means they're midway through resurfacing the road so they've taken away the top layer/s but left the *sinks* standing proud.

Spell.   In *Me Sannies* I discussed the use of the word spell as a noun meaning a splinter of wood or metal that gets stuck into your skin, often associated with mild (in women) and excruciating (in men) pain. This use of the word is a Hull expression though in use occasionally elsewhere. The spell I'm describing here is a verb as in *we'll spell each other* meaning we'll take turns doing something. It seems to have its origins in an old English word

gespelia which can be loosely translated as *substitute*. It wouldn't
fit into the song by The Who but, hey. Apparently there are
eleven different meanings of the word spell, some universal – for
example in a game of cricket someone might have a good *spell* of
bowling – which is quite close in its meaning to the Hull *We'll spell
each other* that I mentioned just now - and others dotted around
the various dialects. Maybe the difference in Hull is that it is a
verb – to spell someone as opposed to a noun - a spell of bowling.
It would seem to have come pretty directly from "gespelia" and is
closely related to the English dialect word "spele," meaning "to
stand in another's place; to represent."

Taking a flyer.   This is an interesting one as it seems to be
one of those expressions that are used in Hull differently from
how they are in the rest of the English-speaking world. To the
rest of the people out there, if you take a flyer, you are taking a
chance, mostly with an investment. Not in Hull. Oh No. Here,
to take a flyer means to leave work early or at very least bang on
time – usually because you have something important to go to.
I'm taking a flyer tonight as City are at Home.

Thee.   No not the old English (or broad West Yorkshire word
for You. This is one that I referred to earlier and I'm pretty sure
that this is a pronunciation issue rather than an actual word but
who's counting? It's used where one might otherwise say there.
As in, for example *Is thee a chippy down Beverley Road* or *Thee
isn't a chippy round here is thee?* For some reason I quite like this.

It has a kind of cousin in the word me which is used all over the country instead of *my*. How many people might say *I haven't brought me coat with me?* I know I do!

Trimmings. Christmas decorations – this appears to have evolved from the expression *to trim* the tree which meant to decorate it but in Hull the decorations themselves have become known as trimmings. This is, of course, not to be confused with *Roast Turkey with all the trimmings*, which describes a Christmas dinner, the trimmings being the vegetables, pigs in blankets, sauces etc. that make up a (sometimes very) full plate.. Only in Hull could we have one word meaning two entirely different things that occur at the same time. You wouldn't put baubles and fairy lights on a plate would you?... Would you? Or sprouts on a tree. Actually I wouldn't put sprouts anywhere.

Underskirt. This is a piece of women's clothing which, thank goodness, has gone completely out of fashion. It's what is, or was, worn under a dress or a skirt and, whereas a skirt is generally from the waist (or hips I suppose) downwards and a dress comes (shall we be discreet and say) further up, you don't get an underdress, you get a full-length underskirt. If you watch The Railway Children (and, nothing at all to do with Hull or its dialect, watching it should be compulsory) you will see the girls stopping a train by waving their red petticoats. That's the more traditional word for it but in many parts of the country it is called a slip. This causes more problems though as a type of men's underpants are now referred to as slips, at least in the well-known chain stores that sell such things.

CHAPTER EIGHT

WORDS WE DON'T USE
(aka the controversial bit of the book)

Allegedly we don't like the word Humberside. There was a huge stink kicked up when local government reorganisation created a new county with that name in 1974. A huge amount of money was spent re-labelling things and twenty-five years later an even bigger amount was spent again re-labelling things to the names of the current 4 so-called Unitary Authorities. All this was because a proportion of the population didn't like the name and another proportion said there was no such place. Nobody in government, national or local, seemed to understand that, if they'd just renamed the actual authority, which was working quite well, they could have saved a large amount of money, if only of senior people's salaries which are based on the number of people living in the area. For example a salary of (say) £100.000 in East Yorkshire and a similar sized one in Hull would equate to one of about £90.000 in what is now North Lincolnshire and about £80,000 in North East Lincolnshire. One for Humberside would have been about £120,000 a saving of about a quarter of a million pounds. Was that another rant?

Anyway, to the point, BBC Radio Humberside existed before 1974 and I don't know whether they had prior knowledge of the proposed change. More to the point , though, as I mentioned earlier, my research took me one day to the Hull Daily Mail for 2 July 1935 when, amongst other things, there was a report of Amy Johnson being injured in a car crash as well as the Sham Four being offered for rent. There was also a reference to a feature called "Humberside Echoes", which commented on everything from the price of wheat to the wedding of a former Hull City footballer with a reference to the "excessive" amount spent on maintaining the roads in Hull. I probably need not comment on anything I've referred to on these two paragraphs other than the fact that the word Humberside had been invented well before any boundary changes came into use.

CONCLUSION

Well that's about as far as I'm going to get with my second volume of rambling about what I'm going to call loving appreciation of the way Hull people speak; or at least those Hull people who speak with the Hull accent and/or dialect.

I do need to thank a number of people. Family and friends of course – my wife Lesley, our grown-up children Carolyn, Martin and Anita along with James, Eleanor and Matt who all regularly find ideas or new words, phrases or expressions for me to research. Some they hear and question; others they just remember or they crop up in conversation and I'll say, "What on earth does that mean", or words to that effect.

Lots of people have contacted me – mostly by Email but some by phone, by letter or even in person. Please forgive me if you're not on this list.

Les Ball; Andy Bareham; Malcolm Bryant; Angela Clark; Joe Clark; Jeannie Coupland; Kevin Crabb; Mark Derbyshire; Amanda Fields; Ian Foster; Alec Gill; Angela Green; Simon Green; Stuart Griffiths; Shirley Hare; Katie Kingsbury; Jo Lewis; Dave Longstaff; Mike Lund; Paula McIntosh; David Mell; Mike O'Brien; Jenny Ramsden; Sylvia Rocke; Paul Schofield; Sue & Steve Smith; Dave Wise; Graham Wood.

DON'T FORGET YER SANNIES!

Thanks to all those people; also to the Town Crier, Michael Wood, for his contributions to this book; to Paul Dennis who made publication possible; and to Steve of Spin-it Records in Hull Market, Julie of Vanilla in Hessle Square, Debbie at Coffee 31, Chris at the Hull People's Memorial, Alice and Joe at Form on Humber Street in Hull, Prue at Traenerhaus and, last but not least, various members of staff at Waterstones in Jameson Street, Hull, all of whom helped me sell *Me Sannies*. Also Sue and Steve Smith and Mandy Nicholson, who allowed me to sell books on their market stalls and, more recently, the people at Dove House Hospice, with whom I am privileged to have a partnership. Then there are the people on Facebook who, every so often recommend or extol the virtues of *Me Sannies are Brannies*. I'd love to think all these people will do the same for this book too.

I mustn't forget Simon Green from Hull Libraries. We'd met a few years earlier on the Hullness project and we met again at a function when I was promoting *Me Sannies*. Following our discussion he sent me a list of words that people claimed to be special to Hull. A fair bit of the research in this book is thanks to information that Simon gave me for which I am grateful.

A special mention, too, for Richardson's Printers in Hull who not only did the setting up and printing but were happy to store several boxes at a time when there wasn't room for them either in our house or Paul Dennis's studio.

DON'T FORGET YER SANNIES!

Oh and also to all those people who have asked me to do talks on the subject - possibly the most difficult task of all and certainly the one least natural to shy little me.

Other people that I know have helped me in other ways. I think in particular of Mike Riding and Kevin Evans and Joan and Brian Butler.

Thanks to all of you. It's been a lot of fun!